Departures

poems by

Allan Johnston

Finishing Line Press
Georgetown, Kentucky

Departures

This collection is for Guillemette

ACKNOWLEDGMENTS

Some of these poems have been previously published, perhaps in slightly different form. I would like to thank the following journals for previously accepting these works:

Bloomsday 2012 & Ulysses' 90th website, *Caesura, Dickinson Review, Evansville Review, Fogged Clarity, Lazy Bones Review, Mid American Poetry Review, Poetry East, Poetry Repairs, Rhino, Segue, Visions International,* and *Weber Studies.* I would also like to thank *Ginosko* for reprinting some of these poems.

Editor: Christen Kincaid

Cover Art: Guillemette Johnston

Author Photo: Guillemette Johnston

Cover Design: Elizabeth Maines

Printed in the USA on acid-free paper.
Order online: www.finishinglinepress.com
also available on amazon.com

Author inquiries and mail orders:
Finishing Line Press
P. O. Box 1626
Georgetown, Kentucky 40324
U. S. A.

TABLE OF CONTENTS

Dawn

A socialist health takes hold of the adult,
He is stripped of his class in the bathing-suit,
He returns to the children digging at summer,
A melon-like fruit.
                    —Delmore Schwartz, "Far Rockaway"

                              The first boat
out in the water bobs along in the breaking up
of the surface, and holds the course loosely,
battered by waves but seeming to have
as its end a movement toward sunrise:

an orange-yellow, flat, plate-like recurrence
of light on the water encrusted with mist.
The sky has not even started to yellow
or blue, but retains its dull grayish wall-like

plaster of fog the light cuts through,
and so is seeming to come from nowhere
if not sudden. These boaters have brought
with them the expectation and the non-

expectation, the gear and the knowledge
that beneath this, there is something or nothing,
that non-directing is an aspect of life
as singing is a reversal for fish,

as lovely as drowning, but one never thinks
of that—The father is talking to his boys
with a fog of cigarette smoke as haze-bound
as the sun. His gear is as netted

and intricate as the mess he must work through
every morning, and so brings survival
into this instant of not really looking
forward, for the boat moves by happenstance,

water buffeting it in continuous
resettings of its non-direction
which is relying upon the sameness
and generosity of the sea.

What after all are destinations
for the entangling schools of fish
or wheeling, eyeing gulls, except
a moment of eating from the waters?

Childhood Near Hollywood

Every day above us
the sun languished, lazing its way
across the sky like some skimpy
bikini-clad model on a tire.

We pictured sunglasses on the sun
to let it keep its glare to itself

but even then we suspected
its need to drink in sustenance
and so drew a stream
between sun and ocean
then hooted with laughter
as children do
and drew sex organs on the sun

then in a frenzy my little brother
scribbled across everything

and yelled out, "Los Angeles!"
The room filled with the screaming clutter

of every street corner god or huckster.
By now we were mad.
We were running around
tearing up pictures: the sun and moon
we had been drawing that afternoon

when my brother yelled "cut!"
and we started with scissors
along the curtains
and then the veneer
of the antique Italian desk. Left alone

we children were terrors, and would not atone
for our actions, or acting.

It all had to end when mother called.

We went out and piled in the station wagon,
leaving our small disaster.
When evening approached, waving flags of surrender,
we grew up and left,
yet still the sea

surrenders its life up to a sun
that boils each heaven to a bone.

Pacific Palisades

That place teetered like a grandmother.
It seemed a mix of ash and flesh—
color, sentiment, and ancient sea.

I, a child climbing that face,
knew nothing about those cliffs
not found through finding and losing footing—

only how the coast formed
its hazard there, and fell toward oceans
in soft moldings of debris.

Here and there, random patches
of buried highway peeked from detritus
near the chain link fence

past which construction of the new road
continued beside a chameleon ocean
always changing, according to the sky.

What were these weathering fabulations
of mud? Hard enough to scramble on;
they powdered underfoot;

the scree slid as you plunged down
into the wreckage of the coast,
a soft announcement of the mountains

rising at the far end of the plateau.
Each year the rain cut off slices of cliff,
trying to push the sea away,

but water was always smarter and had
no sense of shame. It waited across the highway
while the road crews cleared out the rubble,

and above, the demolition teams
took down the houses left dangling over
or too near the drop for habitation.

That place was terraces, yarrow, chaparral,
clad in sunlight, a rough skin of cracking mud,
a constellation of pebbles in clay

that, like a grandmother, spent days remembering
how the land and sea had once kissed.

Piers

The wastages and way stations of the ocean
take the coast in small denominations.
POP, a tropical island themed park
where at the end, in a semblance of volcano,
we'd ride small train cars out over the water,
has washed away, its wreckage clearly rendered
in the surfing scenes of *Lords of Dogtown.*
The pier at Santa Monica, more stable
perhaps, or calling for a deeper investment
for its boat moors, has since gone all touristical.
No more is it just a place to catch fish
with carny stalls and a famous carrousel.
At one time I would find the hidden niches
to cast my line from, pulling up small bass
and a few other fry, but I was no fisherman,
and never stomached gutting as well as I could.
At pier's end the boats unloaded their catch,
freight carts of fish kept chilled with blocks of ice,
on second-layer levels by the boat house.
Below the pier, amongst the staggered pylons,
druggies and queers rendezvoused. But what did I know
then of this? The few times fishing, the thousand walks
along the pier to its facing toward the water
then back, brings back to mind all I remember
of life along the ancient palisade,
the disappearing city of my youth.
Beside the California Avenue incline
the ruins of an old hotel, ornamented
in grand Egyptian frippery, had left
only the imprint of its swimming pool,
a large terra cotta colored basin
filled with the glyphs of Isis and Osiris,
and home to rubble and old shopping carts
pushed from the cliffs above in delinquent joy.
As Jeffers says, in the few thousand years
that sees the decimation of all cities
perhaps a few cascades of stone will linger,

signs of the more important monuments
of *homo fiduciarius.* But still
will stay the overall layout of the coast,
the eating ocean, solid in its ambivalence,
forever taking and depositing,
and rendering the rhythms of the coast
in the continuous music of its washing
as wave hits shore and pylon, carrying all
with its incessant beat: wave, wave, wave, wave.

Visiting Grandmother

I'd sit beneath the Italianate cabinet,
flicking the hanging handles of the drawers—

each one a flowered loop and tit
with an arabesque piercing of brass. I could handle

this fascination, thoughtless metallic
working;
        clack, clack, they sang on antique plackets

joined to the cherry dark wood. The pitches
differed, one a half-tone higher.

My grandmother, in lace frock and black, tight necklace
with a small cameo at the front,

said that I looked like Troy Donahue.
She was speaking to my father.

He had brought me, kid-blonde and awkward,
down coast to see her in her beachside apartment

filled with the burnish of her life.
She was passing out of existence.

     Driving home,
safe on the back seat
of the Plymouth coupe,

the tires humming on the scored coastal road,
I would start to enter the world of sleep
that keeps pitching back on itself,

where dream
and waking become the same. My grandmother,
pale as the small ghost housed in the cameo egg at her throat,

would speak to me
of the dreams of the world that we all are leaving,

that cannot be explained. I was riding
up to the coast on a wave as Troy Donahue
might surf his way to another beginning
TV series. This was the shape

of consciousness. Her smile grew red
with lipstick, her chin forming a canyon
of cracked, ridged flesh that was now easing
into the brooch, and the pink-pale face

of the cameo kept on looking sideways
into an even more distant world.

The Unstrung Bow

Past Sunset, Bienvenida
curled between the blocks of houses
lining the canyon bottom,
then rose slightly
to St. Matthew's school and parish.
Here I, early on,
gained my first enculturation,
passed through preschool. Soon the teachers
started sending notes home.
I was declared "eccentric,"
mainly because, during recess,
rather than play with the other children,
I would take the unstrung bow
now become a child's toy
and climb the canyon side
to one of the sandstone crags
rising from the chaparral.
There I, Indian in my mind,
would watch my running, screaming
schoolmates spread across the lawn
of the church ground. Somehow I
still feel I learned more
about whatever deity
or force might reign by sitting on
those rocks than I ever learned
in the church or school.

Faces

A rust of red sandstone, a silk outcropping,
lay past the pavement's edge that year,
its bare face lifting below
the bite the landslide took from the road.
Yarrow and sagebrush clumped some yards
farther down, then it all plunged
toward cracked, brittle courses
with curled old parchments of mud
dried in the washed-out gullies.

We called it the land of a thousand faces,
for soon that summer the children
started carving the pliant sandstone,
drawn as if by custom.

First came trenches for plastic soldiers,
then came the faces—demons, pirates, clowns,
then sphinxes and strange arabesques
until the silt seemed to pock in kinship

with the sediments of the mountains,
equally marked, another history,
where pebbles that reach the sea
roll out, leaving holes
in the eyeless land,
soft breakings from deep slopes
into what washes away.
We scrambled on the escarpment,
bearing toys and talismans.

Then winter came. Storms reeled from the tropics.
In long days at school,
protected while waters hurled outside,
I thought of how Gods have a way

of passing, of how Jesus
said he could save us
if we were good
enough.
                    After one storm,
the cliff fell toward waters.

That Sunday, at church, the preacher
spoke of houses built on sand.

Flight

for my father

It is again as it is
in the places that I have left
before night falls, and I sit
in the configuration
of stars and the lights of aircraft passing
away from the city into the blue
and blackening sky that stretches farther
than I have ever given thought
to wander. My father, hand
on the back porch railing,
wants it to be as it is;
I can see him looking
into the deepening well
of darkness. I can see
the way his fingers fidget
along the cool, black iron
of the banister.
If he could speak, I know
he would mention the chance
that summer could be here,
that we could be coming home
to sit together again.
I know he would be looking
for a way to tell me
that he is happy or sorry
for everything, for the way
night brings its dark wing
over us, and the distant lights
of aircraft blink down
to the orange edge of the day
that is quietly dying
into the black of the sea.
He would like to think of the way
an aircraft becomes a star,
filled with the luck of horizons
until there is no going home.

Livorno

The house where we lived near cliffs
in dark places of undreamed growth
itself trails out of nothingness
to the grass slope from the door
of the house on Livorno Street.
Light dances on paint and stucco,
pink fresh and warm brick. We moved there
from where the cliff dropped suddenly

beyond the fence at the end of the yard
to Sunset. There eucalyptus
lined the road; one nameless house,
the green room, then to the street called Livorno.

Three to a queen bed, we children nudged
one another with elbows. It had to be
that one would fall through the dream light
of the room to the floor, rise and cry.
I looked. Brother and sister lay warm,
stuffed bear and Candy Indian Chief doll
tucked under arms. Then we moved
to Livorno, high in the child's eye;

sunlight, pink brick, honey-colored stucco,
lawn in the back yard and sleepy trees
under phone lines that ran to horizons.
The church an easy walk, death known
only in the small round of robin egg
found by a tree.
                    Livorno: lazy name;
a child's shout, now as distant as the harbor
of our birth where sailors stilettoed
in silence. I recall rose color,
faces long gone: a neighbor lost at sea;
parents of friends, long since divorced,
sitting up all night, playing guitar,
singing of what happened in Monterrey
a long time ago,
wrapped in afghans, warmed by liquor.
My brother and sister and I;

we punctured sleep with our elbows in the green room
and sudden flights in the unfinished dream space
to wake on floors. Then we moved from the house
where the sudden cliff dropped beyond the fence
at the end of the yard to the boulevard
where eucalyptus lined the road;
nameless house, green room, then to the street
I would call "live-or-no,"
house in the suburbs, pink fresh and warm brick
dancing in light, and the grass slope down
to Livorno Street, itself a trail
out of nothingness;
grown from dark places of undreamed growth,
houses where we lived near cliffs.

Nursery

Swarthmore Avenue ran to the mountains
from the cliffs that faced the sea
and Via de las Olas, the street
edging along the slice of cliff.
I would walk each morning to school,
heading up Swarthmore, passing the house
where one day the drunk raged
as he waved his razor blade
and sliced his arm. Blocks beyond
was Palisades Elementary
with its Spanish-style bell tower.
And there, across the road,
near the telephone building,
stood a nursery, abloom
with coddled flats and terra cotta
pots that dripped with flowers,
dazzling nose and eye.
                              The nursery
offered a pageantry of fuchsia,
snapdragon, and artless fern
to the child's receptive eye
and imagination.
In the foliage near the street
I could engage in recreated
primeval worlds every time
the nurseryman was focused elsewhere.
Those small plots supported dreams
in the dancing play of plastic,
rainbow-shaded one-inch dinosaurs.
Here was a world just as lost
as that massive chasm
in the film of Jules Verne's
Journey to the Center of the Earth

with its nonchalant iguanas
gussed-up like Dimetrodon
and Pat Boone in action, saving
Swede, scientist, and starlet. I
was star-struck, mostly by what
was lost—
                    each flat a misplaced
Amazon, its own brief center
of an earth now stripped of eons,
dinosaurs of every shape
arranged within a frame of flowers
behind the surprising, clouding fact
of the rise and fall of genera,
creation and extinction.

Quick as a breath all was gone;
the child snatching up extinction's
erasures as the nurseryman
plied his way through Swarthmore Nursery.

El Paso

Under the night the child
is opening the window
to his bedroom. Outside,
a rumble of sea and highway
floats in the dark wind from
the canyons to the cliff
the house is hanging on
in the child's mind.

The window is open, the air
is all one side of a world,
a steep drop down the white wall
of the house. The other side
is the bedstead. The radio
sitting on it, small and squat,
quietly, constantly empties itself
of music. It fills with the songs
it produces. It is made
to sing about the lovers
who leave, come back,
and die; he has heard the songs,
and sings along with them in the orange light

of the alarm. The small light seems
like a campfire or a moon
riding high in a laughter of light
over the bedspread, the ghost of the land
the song describes. He sings
in bed alone:

     "Something
is dreadfully wrong, for I feel,"
the words of the song. It's Marty Robbins'
"El Paso," and in the song
the cowboy tumbles, the guitar dances
happily in the orange glow
of the alarm, adrift like a smoke-chased
moon or a child's closing eye.
The song ends, one begins:

"By The Time I Get to Phoenix"—

all lovers leave in the myth, and words
stream into music, make homes out of tune.

Unstopped

For two seconds the brake sticks
and then, in the slip and release,
all is perhaps on a roll
down the street toward the fence and the subtle
cliff, and the children in the car
who in their playing knocked the gear
and brake do not realize
that all glory waits for day
to begin. The game suddenly
moves from distraction to the roll
toward doom, but Hal, our neighbor,
sees the car and runs out.
He catches the door and opens it
and pulls on the emergency brake
before any real speed is gained.
The game is over. The children get out
of the car. Hal goes inside
to tell my father to repark,
and soon the incident
is forgotten.
              Now, years later,
the great steel object of life
rolls without emergency
or brake away from all
those years. Hal is dead.
My father is dead. My brothers
and my sister are scattered across
the continent. We seldom speak
out of absorption with our lives.
I have gone toward my own cliff
that looms on the far side
of play, and for all soaring and grinding,
death is bearing down on us all
like a runaway car.

Walnuts
   for Kevin Clark

Here from the top it all made sense:
how the white Spanish walls between
the houses met, the geometry
of neighborhoods squared out into lines.
I'd sit in the tree for hours
looking through leaves and coffee-stain berries
down the block and toward the cliff
that dropped to the ocean, clouds, and sky,
and sense the peace of it all,
the parceling out of the land,
the way each life could spend
 its brief, green section of grass;
Old Man Wilson with his mulch-pile,
the Winslows further, the house always closed
to the yard, and the Granitellis
next door, with a green lattice flower house
they never used, a part of the property
now the province of German Shepherds
that would take a hand off of you
before you could retrieve a ball.
It wasn't walnuts, there were no walnut trees
as there are here, it was just a tree,
and they were the neighbors, and it all seems
so vast and old, so far and dying.

The Roses

The garden was never so distant as now
when I smell it here, twenty years after
the night I was ten years old
and slept with my friend on the driveway
leading to the backyard;
"did you ever do it," he asked.
I, too young or hidden to answer
or even know, peered out of my sleeping bag
toward the roses that heaved up
out of the dirt smudging itself
down a concrete wall that faced
the city; my love light lost
in solitude somewhere in
another nameless state,
I could only give back ignorance
as the heart-struck angels and apostles
gathered around a throne of roses,
an empty chair of gold
where a young, blond, blue-eyed Jesus
someday would sit, his eyes burnt to nothingness
by his father's desert;
"no," I said, "no," the only answer
bubbled in the red sea of my veins
in the continuing silence of concrete;
I am buried in roses, my heart standing still.

Shell

The sea is always giving up on land.
It leaves reminders, bears the principal,
deposits interest; in this case, a shell
that long since winked away from life, enjambed

Its clever creature's wrinkle out of water
into some hard and horny house, away
from all that water carries in its pay
of particle and current. A strange mother,

The water gives and takes with equal ease.
But now the child who walks the fluent field
where sea and land advance their cache will yield
and reach into the flow, as if to seize

the rapid, foaming treasure of the waves,
but only to identify the shell
that pulls along like paper in a gale.
Feeling it, he moves into a glaze

of interest himself. For now a net
of shy investments binds him to this world
he silently invites, before the curled
reminder of the day is marked and set

in pocket with his other talismans.
He later will arrange them on his bed
as tokens to the moments that have led
the sliding encrustation beyond skin,

the assets that become him. For he builds
a shell from bits and pieces, brings himself
to bear resemblance to this secret gulf
of bonds and certifiers of the wilds

he walks beside. And thus, by giving sense
to life, a self, a shell, he comes to live
by check and balance, counting on what gives
him chance to ebb into this difference.

Octopus

Under rocks washed with tides,
we children would sometimes find
a soft, chameleon octopus,
tentacled up and exaggerated
in its whisper of something
as close as life in the sea permits;
low oxygen levels
bearing on everything we call thoughts
or feelings, carrying all
about on its own in this different world,
water, with what we would call
deep reds of intention
flushing over the body, or cool
cucumber greens of solitude
considering what to do next,
this sly aquatic cat:

three hearts pump the copper-based
blood through the slow, lovely
push-push of sex and death.
Increasingly complex,
the octopus calculates all,
rehearses the imperative
for distant, landed cousins.
For the sea starves off the need to skim
objectively after tasks or things;
what is, floats by: the copulant,
the lounger, dinner, registered
in this reduced activity.
Strange bedfellow, the octopus:
waiting for lunch to catch up,
spreading the egg or seed just once,
then dying; sending off a ghost
of him-slash-herself, and so escaping
everything, wailing away
with eight legs through the water, leaving
a phony reference—completely disjointed,
the predators fooled by ink;
it slinks to the deep, slime soft, slippery,
this sly aquatic body.

Radishes
Paul Revere Junior High School, 1962

Flames shot orange tatters over the long stone
bounds of the Santa Monica Mountains
hanging above us. The heavy clouds
of smoke from the burning chaparral
became a nut-brown choke of savory
fragrances that blurred the world
for days.
                    And in other ways
the world turned on us. Once when rains
played on the hills for days, washing
out the ash-grey and fire-stripped slopes,
we joined in the rescue effort,
stacking sand bags to protect
the basketball court of the junior high,
the long green course of the runners.
All throughout that first semester in seventh
grade, before the sun hit the plot,

I took a horticulture class
first period. I was growing
radishes on the small hillock
under the house we knew for its windows.
They never closed, a sure sign of haunting.
Mr. Long, the teacher,
an ex-Marine, was ready to go
on call with his reserve unit
as Vietnam heated.

One cold morning I planted the seeds,
and each day I came to see
what had grown in the rows
of my tiny miracle.
But it being just another semester
of early mornings for me,
my slow plot only brought forth
radishes I would not harvest
until much later,
in some sort of sudden flash
of recollection after so many years.

I find them now, again, and just now
know to harvest what was begun.

High School Biology Class, 1965

Mr. Small, in his white lab coat,
seemed like a stout albino pygmy.

He would watch with beady eyes
as the girls and the over-wealthy,

swishy guy *eewed!* with disgust
at the neatly dissected frog,

skin pinned down each way to show
the lungs, the guts, and the small wad of heart.

All the jocks in class kept guffawing.
They were clowning about, imitating

the girls and the guy with effeminate swishes,
prime meat for their aggression.

I meanwhile turned back to the deep,
descending jungles of gold lichen

shimmering in the petri dish
under the gilded knobs and tackle

of the stereo microscope.
I'd twiddle down through the narrow focus

of its walls and canyons with the dials.
Down there, in the evocative world

of that strange, fantastic realm,
small accumulations of life

seemed as ardent as the tension
of the jocks who mocked the girlish.

Gone Too Far Near Singing

The way light may weigh on sense
or seal the gesture of the land,

or how a scene may slip in sunset
into pools of gestures;

these are words where afternoons
can read their presence into night.

They say how songs can captivate
a landscape; worlds of dragonflies

then weave between the undulations
of the cattails raised from water

now in how it all retrieves us.
Then we see too closely in

the world to get away. Thought ends.
We find ourselves

gone too far near singing not
to be the sound of breath.

Home Before Dark

There are ways
Across dark fields
Breaking open with flower
At sundown;

Ways to encase
The sensation
That the moon rides high
On its laugh
Of light.

This is the road
Before sundown,
And there are ways
In every sense

To lose yourself
Before dark
While somewhere across fields
Home is hiding.

Waking

This ceramic slip of sky
holds a moon
too still to be real
a moon you have dreamt of
and yet not that moon
an egg cup of sleep
that laughs in the soft wash
of dawn
    your hand
moves out of sleep
to your mouth   there are cobwebs
on the window
light falls through the room
and beyond
uncut fields of grass
bring joy to birds

it is of this
you have been dreaming
the moon that shimmers
the unnecessary moon
in eaves where swallows
glide in light
and spiders whisper
out the whims
of their webs

clouds bleed
over scars of mountains

we roll and touch in sleep
in this way we waken

Departures

Picture the wicker of the rippled water
as he remembers it, or recall
the surface burnished smooth as stone, the weather
easy as a summer ought to be;
easy as the liquor in the glass
through which the table's curvature distorts
into a bulging eye, or else an egg
forever unbroken. After it passes the lip,
the loud song of vodka in the mouth
details another moment of departure,
another salutation to the missing
that brings him back across the continent
to face again the place where waves slap down
and splash the land below the orange-brown cliffs
he'd climb down to reach the sea and find her
mottled in foam and in memoranda of driftwood,
in the Hottentot fig and coastal flowers
that open spiked heads outward toward water.
On the bicycle path he'd follow homeward
past the fields where deer feed in wild wheat,
the black heads of grasses sway in breezes
before you and behind you. If you remember
the waves of grass, if you recall the sound
of birds as they chirp their hopelessness,
if you recall the seed of loss that opened
in his voice, the dream of the second person,
then you know the time is ripe for departure,
for the land between us is as real
as the brief stretch of my hand before my eye,
and yet as ineffaceable as stone,
as insistent as the patterning of water,
and as hard as the broken love that comes between us.